HARD AS NAILS IN

Ancient Greece

TRACEY TURNER

ILLUSTRATED BY JAMIE LENMAN

Crabtree Publishing Company
www.crabtreebooks.com

Crabtree Publishing Company
www.crabtreebooks.com
1-800-387-7650

616 Welland Ave.
St. Catharines, ON
L2M 5V6

PMB 59051, 350 Fifth Ave.
59th Floor,
New York, NY

Published by Crabtree Publishing Company in 2015.

Author: Tracey Turner

Illustrator: Jamie Lenman

Project coordinator: Kelly Spence

Editors: Becca Sjonger

Proofreader: Robin Johnson

Prepress technician: Tammy McGarr

Print coordinator: Margaret Amy Salter

Copyright © 2014 A & C Black

Text copyright © 2014 Tracey Turner

Illustrations copyright © 2014 Jamie Lenman

Additional illustrations © Shutterstock

Printed in Canada/022015/MA20150101

First published 2014 by
A & C Black, an imprint of
Bloomsbury Publishing Plc.

Library and Archives Canada Cataloguing in Publication

Turner, Tracey, author
    Hard as nails in ancient Greece / Tracey Turner ; illustrated by Jamie Lenman.

(Hard as nails in history)
Includes index.
ISBN 978-0-7787-1512-2 (bound).--
ISBN 978-0-7787-1515-3 (pbk.)

    1. Greece--Biography--Juvenile literature.
2. Greece--History--Juvenile literature. I.
Lenman, Jamie, illustrator II. Title.

DF208.T87 2015   j938   C2014-908090-5

Library of Congress Cataloging-in-Publication Data

Turner, Tracey.
 Hard as nails in ancient Greece / Tracey Turner ; Illustrated by Jamie Lenman.
    pages cm. -- (Hard as nails in history)
 Includes index.
 ISBN 978-0-7787-1512-2 (reinforced library binding : alk. paper) -- ISBN 978-0-7787-1515-3 (pbk. : alk. paper)
1. Greece--History--To 146 B.C.--Biography--Juvenile literature. 2. Greece--History--146 B.C.-323 A.D.--Biography--Juvenile literature.
I. Lenman, Jamie, illustrator. II. Title.

DF208.T97 2015
938.009'9--dc23
                                    2014046716

CONTENTS

TO
ATHENS

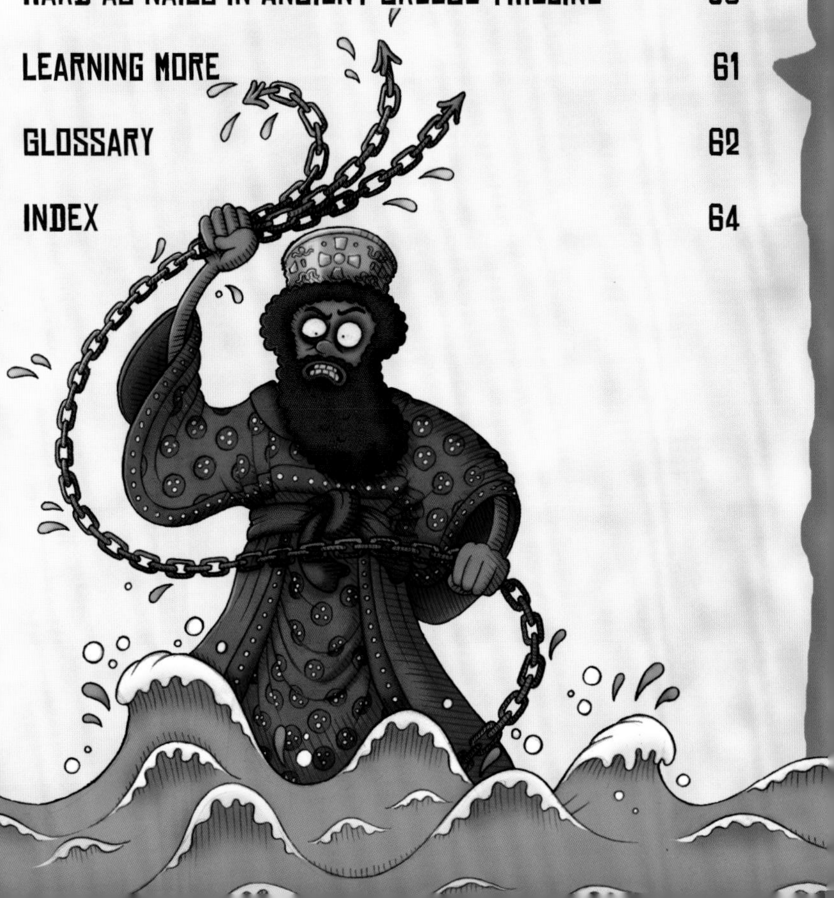

INTRODUCTION

This book describes some of the toughest men and women in ancient Greek history, from brave Spartan warriors to pondering Athenian philosophers. Some of them were courageous, some were clever, some were fearsome, and some were absolutely awful. But they all were as hard as nails.

FIND OUT ABOUT . . .

• An ancient family curse

• Cruel, power-crazed tyrants

• A nine-headed water snake

• Burning death rays that set fire to ships

If you've ever wanted to discover the meaning of life, join the powerful Spartan army, or invade Sicily, read on. Follow along on the first marathon ever, to the bloody battlefields of the Peloponnese, and aboard a Persian warship in the Mediterranean Sea.

As well as discovering stories of courage and cunning, you might be in for a few surprises. Did you know, for example, that Alexander the Great named a city after his horse? Or that Persian King Xerxes was so cross with the sea that he had it whipped with chains?

Get ready to meet some of the toughest people in ancient Greece. . .

Plus take the quiz on page 22 and find out what type of ancient Greek philosopher you are.

7

CLEISTHENES

Cleisthenes became famous for his politics, but first he had to battle a power-crazed tyrant, a ruthless rival, and an ancient family curse.

HARD AS NAILS RATING: 7.5

CLEISTHENES'S CURSE

Cleisthenes was born in Athens around 570 BCE into a well-off family, which, unfortunately, had a curse upon it. Cleisthenes's great-grandfather had killed political rivals after they took refuge in a temple, breaking his promise to keep them safe. As a result, Cleisthenes's family was cursed and thrown out of Athens. They were eventually allowed back, but then got kicked out again because of the curse.

HIPPIAS THE TYRANT

Hippias was the tyrant of Athens. In those days, "tyrant" meant an absolute ruler, like a king. It didn't necessarily mean a cruel megalomaniac—but in Hippias's case, it did. Cleisthenes and his extended family managed to get rid of horrible Hippias. But then Cleisthenes was sent into exile by his political rival Isagoras and his Spartan friends. The excuse for getting rid of Cleisthenes was the family curse, which came back to haunt him again.

HARDOMETER

CUNNING: 9
COURAGE: 7
SURVIVAL SKILLS: 8
RUTHLESSNESS: 6

ISAGORAS GETS NASTY

Isagoras made himself very unpopular, partly by announcing that various families were cursed and sending them into exile. After all, it had worked so well with Cleisthenes. Isagoras also tried to get rid of a long-established Athenian council. The people of Athens decided they wanted Isagoras out, so they rioted. They trapped Isagoras and his supporters on the Acropolis and ruthlessly killed most of them, but Isagoras managed to escape. Cleisthenes was called back to Athens and elected archon, the top job in Athenian politics.

CLEISTHENES TAKES CHARGE

Cleisthenes decided to make things fairer and change the way Athens was run. He divided people into groups according to where they lived instead of family ties, and made other changes like reorganizing the courts of law. He also introduced the idea of equal rights for all. His changes encouraged more people to become involved in politics than ever before. After he died, Cleisthenes became known as "the father of Athenian democracy."

EXILE

GREEK CITY-STATES

The people who lived in ancient Greece didn't call themselves ancient Greeks—not even the really old people. Instead, they were Athenians, Spartans, or groups from one of the other Greek city-states. (The Greek name for a city-state is "polis," which is how we get the word "politics.")

The ancient Greeks all spoke the same language, and had the same religion and myths, so they shared a lot in common. Sometimes they joined together to fight a common enemy, and sometimes they fought one another. The two most powerful city-states during Greece's Classical Age were Athens and Sparta.

ATHENS

Athens had an unusual (for ancient times) system of government: citizens were ruled by elected leaders and had a say in how they were governed. In fact, it was expected that all Athenian citizens would take an active role in government and law. Not everyone was a citizen, though. Women, foreigners, and slaves (and there were a lot of these) were not considered citizens.

SPARTA

Sparta was ruled by two kings and a council of elders, and had the most powerful army in all of Greece. Male Spartan citizens were trained to be especially tough fighters. Like Athens, Sparta relied on slaves. Spartan slaves were called "helots," and once a year it was acceptable for Spartans to kill them! It's no wonder they sometimes rebelled. Sparta and Athens joined together with several other Greek city-states to fight against Persian invaders, but battled each other in the Peloponnesian War.

OTHER CITY-STATES

There were hundreds of other city-states throughout Greece. Corinth was a wealthy city-state. It was on the same side as Sparta in the Peloponnesian War, but later fought against Sparta. Syracuse, a city on the island of Sicily, was a Corinthian colony. The city-state of Thebes joined forces with the Persians when they invaded Greece in 480 BCE, but fought with Sparta against Athens in the Peloponnesian War. Thebes defeated Sparta and became the most powerful city-state in ancient Greece in the 300s BCE.

ALEXANDER THE GREAT

Alexander the Great was a rampaging conqueror who founded dozens of cities, defeated an empire, and created an enormous new one of his own.

KING ALEXANDER

Alexander's father, King Philip II of Macedonia, was assassinated in 336 BCE. Alexander, who was 20 years old, became king. Philip had made Macedonia powerful: it controlled most of Greece and had a huge, well-trained army. After Philip's death, Alexander began his reign by killing his father's murderers and any rivals to the throne, and ruthlessly crushing a Greek uprising in Thebes. But Alexander didn't stop there: he had big plans for expansion.

BATTLING THE PERSIANS

Darius III ruled the mighty Persian Empire, which stretched from Asia Minor (modern-day Turkey) around the Mediterranean and into Egypt. Alexander tried to take the empire for himself at the Battle of Issus. Alexander's army battered the Persians, even though the Persian army was more than twice the size of his. Darius ran away, but he met Alexander again at the Battle of Gaugamela. This time, Alexander defeated the Persians completely, and he was proclaimed Great King of Asia.

HARDOMETER

CUNNING: 8
COURAGE: 8
SURVIVAL SKILLS: 8
RUTHLESSNESS: 9

CONQUERING EVERYONE ELSE

Alexander marched into Babylon next, where he did a lot of celebrating, then on to Susa, the capital city of Persia (modern-day Iran), gathering treasure as he went. He conquered his way through central Asia and into what's now Pakistan and India. In India, he defeated King Porus, whose army rode into battle on elephants. But by this time, Alexander's army felt that they'd done enough conquering and wanted to go home, so they turned back.

NO MORE CONQUERING

By the end of Alexander's conquering days, his huge empire stretched from the Mediterranean to the Himalayas. He celebrated his victories with massive parties. However, after one party he became ill and died, at the age of just 32. In the 12 years he'd been king, Alexander had founded more than 70 cities. Many of them were called Alexandria, but he named one Bucephalia, after his trusty war horse Bucephalus.

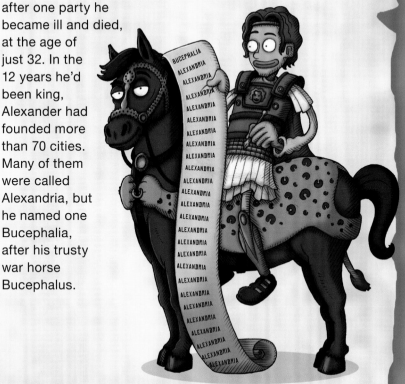

BUCEPHALIA
ALEXANDRIA
ALEXANDRIA
ALEXANDRIA
ALEXANDRIA
ALEXANDRIA
ALEXANDRIA
ALEXANDRIA
ALEXANDRIA
ALEXANDRIA
ALEXANDRIA
ALEXANDRIA
ALEXANDRIA
ALEXANDRIA
ALEXANDRIA
ALEXANDRIA
ALEXANDRIA
ALEXANDRIA
ALEXANDRIA
ALEXANDRIA
ALEXANDRIA
ALEXANDRIA

THE PERSIANS AND THE PELOPONNESE

THE PERSIAN WARS

The Persian Wars began in 499 BCE and lasted until 449 BCE. Persia had a massive empire that stretched from the Mediterranean Sea to the Indus River valley, including Greek cities in Asia Minor and some Greek islands. Greece was next.

Even though Greece was tiny compared to the Persian Empire, Sparta had an army of terrifyingly tough warriors, and Athens had a quick and clever navy that was unbeatable at sea. Other city-states joined them in the fight against the Persians. There were three major battles during the Persian Wars—Marathon, Thermopylae, and Salamis (see pages 46, 16, and 28). In each one, the Persians were thwarted, even if they weren't completely defeated. They never managed to grab Greece.

THE PELOPONNESIAN WAR

Twenty years after the end of the Persian Wars, the Greeks were at it again, this time fighting among themselves. The Peloponnesian War is named after the Peloponnese, the big peninsula that included Sparta and other ancient city-states. They formed the Peloponnesian League, which fought the Athenian Empire from 431 BCE to 404 BCE.

There was an uneasy peace in the middle of the war, but it didn't last long. In the end, Sparta had help from the Persians (them again!), and finally Athens surrendered. Athens never rose to be a great power again, and civil war among the Greek city-states became common. The golden age of ancient Greece was over.

LEONIDAS

Leonidas became legendary for his astonishing courage while defending Greece from the Persians against all odds.

HARD AS NAILS RATING: 7.5

PRINCE LEONIDAS

Leonidas was born in the city-state of Sparta, the son of the Spartan king. Like all well-born Spartan boys, he went to a hard as nails boarding school from the age of seven, where he learned how to be a tremendously tough Spartan warrior. Leonidas became king around 490 BCE.

THOSE PESKY PERSIANS

The Persians wanted to make Greece part of their empire, and had already tried to invade. In 480 BCE, Persian leader Xerxes the Great (see page 48) was plotting another invasion. He had a huge army and navy ready—this time he really meant business. But Leonidas planned to stop the Persians at Thermopylae, a pass between the mountains and the sea. He led an army of allied Greeks into battle.

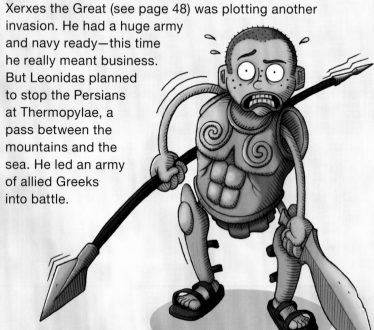

OUTNUMBERED

Leonidas and the Greeks were massively outnumbered, probably by about 10 to one. Leonidas could see that his only chance of stopping the Persians was to defend the narrowest part of the pass. The Persians sent him a message saying something along the lines of, "You and your pathetic little army don't stand a chance—surrender and lay down your weapons." Leonidas replied by saying something like, "Come and get them—if you think you're tough enough."

SECRET PASS

Leonidas and his men were so tough that they held back the huge Persian army. Unfortunately, a sneaky traitor told the Persians about a secret pass through the mountains. When Leonidas discovered he'd been betrayed, he realized that as soon as the Persians got through the secret pass, the Greek army would be massacred. He sent most of the men to safety, then fought on with about 1,500 of his hardest soldiers, all of whom knew they faced certain death.

DEFEAT . . . AND VICTORY

Leonidas and his soldiers all died fighting the Persians. But their bravery and self-sacrifice made them famous. Many Persians also died in the battle, and their army never fully recovered from it. Even though the Persians won, the following year they were sent packing from Greece for good.

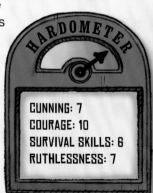

HARDOMETER

CUNNING: 7
COURAGE: 10
SURVIVAL SKILLS: 6
RUTHLESSNESS: 7

LYSANDER

Lysander was the commander of the Spartan fleet that defeated Athens and finally ended the Peloponnesian War.

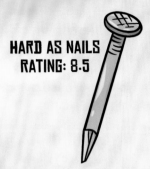

HARD AS NAILS
RATING: 8.5

HUMBLE BEGINNINGS

Lysander's family were Heracleidae, a group of Spartans who claimed their ancestor was the ancient Greek mythical hero Heracles (see page 36). The family must have fallen on hard times, because Lysander needed a rich Spartan sponsor in order to go to the tough military boarding school, called the "agoge," where he learned how to be a hard as nails Spartan warrior.

ADMIRAL OF THE FLEET

Lysander must have done really well because, in 407 BCE he got the top job of "navarch," or admiral, of the Spartan fleet. At the time, the Peloponnesian War was raging between Sparta and Athens. Lysander created a Spartan fleet capable of fighting the mighty Athenian fleet at Ephesus. At the Battle of Notium, he defeated the Athenian (and later Spartan) general Alcibiades (see page 32).

HARDOMETER

CUNNING: 9
COURAGE: 8
SURVIVAL SKILLS: 9
RUTHLESSNESS: 8

LYSANDER FIGHTS AGAIN

Lysander didn't stay in his job for long. After he'd left, the Athenians won a big battle against the Spartan navy, and the Spartans decided they needed Lysander's brilliant leadership again. Spartan law didn't allow the same navarch to hold the job twice, and it was very strict about its rules, so Lysander became deputy admiral. But everyone knew that he was really in charge.

SPARTA WINS

Lysander sailed the Spartan fleet to the Hellespont, a narrow, 37 mile (60 km) stretch of sea that links the Mediterranean with the sea of Marmaris. At the Battle of Aegospotami, Lysander and the Spartans defeated the Athenians. They also captured Byzantium (which is now the city of Istanbul), Chalcedon, and the island of Lesbos. The Spartan king Pausanias besieged Athens, and Lysander's fleet blockaded its port. Athens had no choice: they surrendered, and Sparta won the Peloponnesian War.

NAVARCH

DEPUTY ADMIRAL

SOCRATES

Socrates wasn't a fighter, he was a thinker. He stuck to his principles, even though it meant his own execution.

STONEMASON AND SOLDIER

Socrates was born around 470 BCE. His family wasn't particularly well-off—his mother was a midwife, and his father was a stonemason and sculptor. For a while that's what Socrates did, too. He also served as a soldier in the Athenian army, and according to another philosopher, Plato, he saved the life of Alcibiades (see page 32) during a battle with Corinth.

THINKING

Socrates gave up being a mason when he decided that the most important thing of all was philosophy, or pondering the meaning of life and how to live well. He wandered around Athens talking to people, asking questions, and thinking deep thoughts. Athens was a good place to be a philosopher, because thinking and studying were generally encouraged.

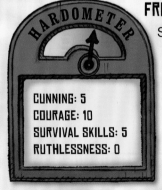

HARDOMETER

CUNNING: 5
COURAGE: 10
SURVIVAL SKILLS: 5
RUTHLESSNESS: 0

FRIENDS AND ENEMIES

Socrates held strong opinions and he wasn't shy about letting everyone know about them. He thought that political leaders should be especially wise, and if he didn't think they were, he said so—loudly. This made him very unpopular with some of the people in charge. He didn't believe in the gods, and he also disagreed strongly with anyone who thought money and physical beauty were the most important things in life. Although he had plenty of friends, he made a lot of influential enemies, too.

HORRIBLE HEMLOCK

Socrates's enemies charged him with being disrespectful to the gods and corrupting young people. Socrates could probably have gotten off the charges if he hadn't stuck to his guns quite so strongly. Instead, he was sentenced to death. His friends were horrified. They offered to bribe the guards and help him escape from Athens—and they would almost certainly have succeeded. But Socrates insisted that he should abide by his principles and the laws of Athens, and took his punishment. He was given poisonous hemlock to drink, and he died.

ANCIENT GREEK PHILOSOPHERS QUIZ

Do you seek truth, wisdom, and the secrets of the universe? Do you question the nature of reality? Want to know everything about . . . well, everything? If so, you should definitely become a philosopher.

The ancient Greeks weren't the first to ask these sorts of questions, but they were the first to put a name to trying to answer them: philosophy, which means "love of wisdom." As well as asking questions about the meaning of life, ancient Greek philosophy included mathematics and science.

The three most famous Greek philosophers are Socrates (see page 20), Plato, and Aristotle. The Epicureans, the Stoics, and the Skeptics were three philosophical ways of thinking about life that came after these men. There were many other kinds, too. Decide which of these ideas about life you most agree with, and find out which kind of philosopher you are.

PLATO

SOCRATES

1 You seek inner peace through moderation in everything. You don't eat too much or work too much, but you don't eat too little or laze around either. You accept what the world gives you rather than striving after things.

2 What can we ever really know about the world, or even about ourselves? And if we don't know much about that, how can we know what's right or wrong? It's better to just relax and leave everything in the hands of the gods.

3 To be happy, it's best not to want anything, because when we can't get what we want it makes us sad. The gods don't really affect people's lives, and when our bodies die our souls do, too, so there's no reason to fear either the gods or death.

If you agree with 1: You're a Stoic. The Stoics were founded by the philosopher Zeno in the 200s BCE. Today, you may be described as "stoic" if you put up with hardship without complaining.

ARISTOTLE

If you agree with 2: You're a Skeptic. Pyrrhon began this kind of philosophy in the 300s BCE. He started from the idea that we can't rely on our senses to tell us the truth about things. Now, a "skeptic" is someone who doubts accepted opinions.

If you agree with 3: You're an Epicurean. Epicurus founded his philosophy in Athens in 307 BCE. The word "epicure" is used today to mean someone who likes gourmet food and drink. However, Epicurus wasn't focused on pleasure, but wanted freedom from pain and anxiety.

HYPATIA

Hypatia was a rare thing in the ancient world—a woman in charge. She was also the leading mathematician and astronomer of her time.

GREECE, EGYPT, AND ROME

Hypatia was Greek, but she was born in Alexandria in Egypt around 355 to 370 CE. By that time Alexandria was part of the Roman Empire, so Hypatia was a sort of Greek-Egyptian-Roman. Her father was a mathematician, and Hypatia became one, too, as well as an astronomer and a philosopher.

HEAD TEACHER

By around 400 CE, Hypatia was head of the Platonist school in Alexandria, a city known for its scholars. Today, we're used to female teachers, but in those days it was extremely unusual. Hypatia must have been a brilliant teacher, as well as hard as nails, to become head of one of the best colleges in the world.

TURBULENT TIMES

HARDOMETER

CUNNING: 5
COURAGE: 9
SURVIVAL SKILLS: 6
RUTHLESSNESS: 5

The governor of Alexandria, Orestes, was constantly arguing with the city's Christian bishop, Cyril. In those days, Christians were angry about having been persecuted for a long time—and some of them (Cyril included) wanted revenge. However, the fights between Cyril and Orestes were really about who was in control of the city. A group of Cyril-supporting monks stormed into Alexandria, and one of them hit Orestes on the head with a rock. Afterward, the monk was tortured to death—and the battle for power became even worse.

MURDER MOST FOUL

A clever woman like Hypatia probably represented everything that was wrong with the world to a lot of the early Christians: she was a non-Christian thinker, a scientist and—perhaps most shocking of all—female! She was also a friend of Orestes's. So, one day in 415 CE, a mob of murderous Christians kidnapped Hypatia and killed her. Her death was extremely gruesome.

ANCIENT GREEK WOMEN

Women in ancient Greece weren't allowed to do the same things as the men, such as giving political speeches, writing plays, becoming philosophers, fighting battles, or getting rich. They weren't even allowed to become citizens or vote. Athenian women—at least, the ones in wealthier homes—even had separate living quarters from the men. They were expected to look after their homes and have children.

SPARTAN GIRL POWER

Things were slightly different in Sparta, where people thought about war first and everything else second. Men had to be tough warriors, and women had to produce boys who'd grow up to be tough warriors. That meant women had to be just as athletic and fit as the men. They were also educated, unlike the girls in Athens. While the men were away (fighting, of course), the women of Sparta had more of a say in running the city-state. Although they still weren't allowed to be citizens, Spartan women could own land, and some of them even became rich.

CHARIOT RACING

Cynisca was a Spartan princess who entered her own chariot team in the Olympic Games—and won, twice (in 396 and 392 BCE). However, she didn't drive it herself (that kind of stuff was still left to the men), even though she was said to be an expert horse rider. She probably wouldn't have even watched her chariot win because there were no women allowed at the Olympics (partly because the men all competed naked). Cynisca was the first woman to win a chariot race, but other women followed in later years.

THEMISTOCLES

Themistocles was an Athenian leader who created and commanded a great navy, and saved Greece from the clutches of the invading Persians.

HARD AS NAILS RATING: 8·5

INVADING PERSIANS

In 493 BCE, when Themistocles was around 31 years old, he was elected chief archon in Athens. Three years later, he was at the Battle of Marathon (see page 46), fighting the huge and terrifying Persian army. The Greeks won and everyone breathed a huge sigh of relief, especially in Athens. Many people thought it was the end of the war. But Themistocles was suspicious.

THEMISTOCLES'S NAVY

Themistocles thought that Athens should make itself invincible at sea, as a defense against the Persians. It wasn't easy, but he managed to persuade the people of Athens to use the money from a newly discovered silver mine to pay for 200 new warships for its navy.

XERXES ATTACKS

Themistocles was right to worry about Persia. The Persian king Xerxes I (see page 48) was planning a second invasion of Greece. At Themistocles's suggestion, the people of Athens were evacuated to the nearby island of Salamis, which could then be protected

HARDOMETER

CUNNING: 9
COURAGE: 9
SURVIVAL SKILLS: 7
RUTHLESSNESS: 9

by the Greek fleet, including the new warships, as well as ships from other Greek city-states.

THE BATTLE OF SALAMIS

The allied Greek navy met the much-larger Persian fleet at Salamis in 480 BCE. But despite the greater number of Persian ships, the Greeks defeated the Persians. The victory was thanks to Themistocles's tactics and the new Athenian warships. It was the beginning of the end of Persia's invasion plans.

THEMISTOCLES GETS THE BOOT

Even though he'd saved Greece from the Persians, Themistocles was accused of conspiring with them and he was exiled. Ironically, he ran away to live in Persian territory, where he became a Persian governor. He died in 462 BCE. One story says that he poisoned himself to avoid having to help the Persians fight against Athens.

ARCHIMEDES

Archimedes is the most famous ancient Greek inventor and mathematician. He was so focused on inventing that he kept working, even when he was in danger from rampaging Roman soldiers.

HARD AS NAILS
RATING: 6.3

GREEKS IN SICILY

Archimedes was born between 290 and 280 BCE in Syracuse in Sicily. He lived there for most of his life. Today, Sicily is part of Italy, but back then it was a Greek city-state. Since it was dangerously close to the capital city of the Roman Empire, the ancient Romans had their eye on it.

NAKED DISCOVERIES

After going to school in Alexandria in Egypt, Archimedes spent the rest of his life exercising his mighty brain on matters such as math and inventing. He's supposed to have invented the Archimedean screw (a device used to raise water), and he came up with the principle of the lever. According to legend, he was having a bath when he made his famous

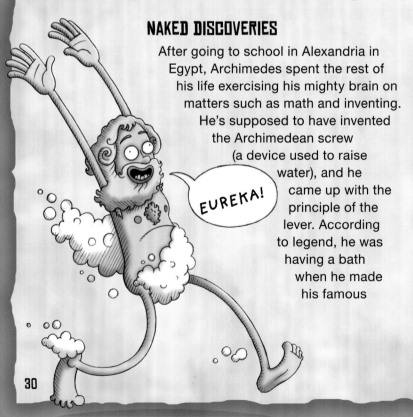

EUREKA!

discoveries about how things float, how much fluid an object displaces, and the weight of the displaced fluid. He's supposed to have shouted "Eureka!" and gone running down the street without any clothes on! The word "eureka" means "I have found it." Today, we use that word when a discovery is made.

ARCHIMEDES'S DEADLY WEAPONS

The Romans attacked Sicily in 214 BCE. Archimedes helped defend Sicily by inventing some cunning weapons of war. These included a catapult and a system of mirrors for focusing the sun's rays on, and setting fire to, invading boats—although the fiery mirrors might be just a story.

ROMAN CONQUERORS

Despite Archimedes's weapons, the Romans won. The story goes that one of the conquering Roman soldiers came across Archimedes on the beach, where he was drawing diagrams in the sand, possibly about to come up with another groundbreaking discovery. Archimedes told the soldier not to disturb his diagram, and the soldier responded by killing him with his sword.

SPHERES AND CYLINDERS

Archimedes's great brain would never come up with another invention or discovery. He was so proud of one discovery—about spheres, cylinders, and their volumes and surface areas—that he asked for a diagram of it to be carved on his tomb.

HARDOMETER

CUNNING: 8
COURAGE: 8
SURVIVAL SKILLS: 5
RUTHLESSNESS: 4

ALCIBIADES

Alcibiades had everything: looks, brains, money—and a tendency to switch sides when things weren't going well!

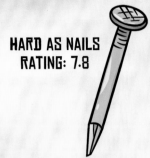

HARD AS NAILS RATING: 7.8

FAMOUS FRIENDS AND FAMILY

Alcibiades was born around 450 BCE in Athens. After his father died, the famous politician Pericles (see page 40) raised him. He grew up to be strong, clever, and amazingly good-looking. He became a friend of the philosopher Socrates (see page 20), with whom he fought bravely in battles between Athens and neighboring city-states.

ATHENIAN ALCIBIADES

Athens and Sparta were at war when Alcibiades became a politician and general. Alcibiades tried and failed to organize an anti-Spartan alliance with other city-states. However, he succeeded in persuading the Athenians to send troops to attack Syracuse in Sicily—a colony of Corinth, Sparta's ally.

DISASTERS

While he was sailing to Sicily, Alcibiades was accused of attacking statues of the gods in Athens and saying rude things about religion. Worse still, the expedition to Sicily turned out to be a total disaster for the Athenians. They were battered, and thousands of soldiers and hundreds of ships were lost. Alcibiades promised to sail back to Athens,

HARDOMETER

CUNNING: 9
COURAGE: 5
SURVIVAL SKILLS: 8
RUTHLESSNESS: 9

but instead sneaked off to help his Spartan enemies, who welcomed him with open arms. Unfortunately, so did the Spartan king's wife, and Alcibiades was exiled from Sparta in 412 BCE.

PERSIA AND ATHENS AGAIN

Alcibiades ran away to Asia Minor which was ruled by Persia, the old enemy of Athens. He contacted the Athenians, promising them money and Persian ships if they would be friendly toward him. Even though he'd betrayed them, the Athenians asked him to come back. He led victories against the Spartans, but in 407 BCE the Athenians exiled him after a defeat in a sea battle.

ALCIBIADES'S END

Alcibiades wasn't in Athens when it met its final defeat by the Spartans in 404 BCE. By then he was in Asia Minor, where he was murdered. No one is sure who killed him—it might have been his old friends the Spartans, or his new ones, the Persians. Swapping sides had finally caught up with him.

DARIUS THE GREAT

Darius the Great grabbed the Persian throne for himself, then began a conquering spree that made the Persian Empire the biggest it would ever be.

HARD AS NAILS RATING: 8.5

DARIUS TAKES CHARGE

Darius was born in 550 BCE, during the reign of another great Persian conqueror, King Cyrus II. Darius was a distant relative of the king, and his father ruled one of the Persian provinces, but Darius had no claim to the throne. When King Cyrus died, his son became king. He was overthrown in 522 BCE, and someone else grabbed the throne. No one today is sure who it was, but according to Darius, he was an evil imposter. So, Darius killed him and took the throne himself.

REBELLIONS

Darius spent several busy years stopping troublesome rebellions that sprang up as a result of the change of ruler. He also wrote laws, fixed taxes, organized currency, built roads, and set up trade routes. But he still found time for empire building. His generals conquered Thrace, Macedonia, the Punjab, and much of the Indus valley. Libya was made a province of the mighty Persian Empire, too.

HARDOMETER

CUNNING: 9
COURAGE: 8
SURVIVAL SKILLS: 8
RUTHLESSNESS: 9

ANGRY GREEKS

In 507 BCE, Darius made an alliance with Athens, but it wasn't long before the Greeks started getting fed up with the Persians. It was pretty obvious that if the Persians had their way, Greece would become part of the Persian Empire, too. In 499 BCE, the Persian Wars—between Persia and allied Greek city-states—began, and carried on for 50 years.

PERSIA INVADES

Darius and his army invaded Greece, and it was nearly 10 years until the Greeks finally got rid of them at the Battle of Marathon (see page 46). Darius began making plans for a second invasion. This time, he planned to fire his generals and take command of the army himself. But in 486 BCE he was stopped—not by the Greeks, but by illness, which killed him.

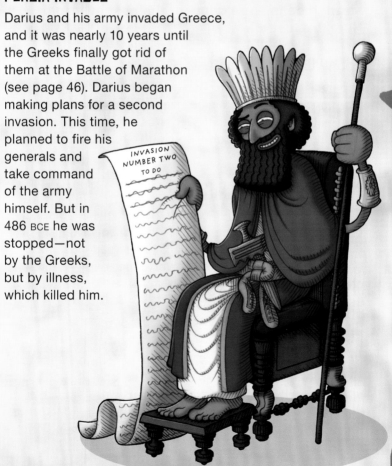

INVASION NUMBER TWO TO DO

ANCIENT GREEK MYTHOLOGY

The ancient Greeks worshiped 12 main gods and goddesses. They included Zeus, king of the gods; Poseidon, god of the sea; Aphrodite, goddess of love; and Athena, goddess of wisdom. In Greek mythology, the gods and goddesses often did bad things, and they were always interfering in human affairs. The ancient Greeks' stories about gods, goddesses, human heroes, monsters, and strange beasts are some of the best ever told. Here are just a few:

THE 12 LABORS OF HERACLES

The gods punished heroic Heracles by giving him 12 tricky tasks, including killing a nine-headed water snake; stealing man-eating horses; getting Cerberus, the three-headed guard dog, from the underworld; and capturing monstrous bulls, boars, and deer.

THESEUS AND THE MINOTAUR

Theseus, prince of Athens, killed the hideous Minotaur, a bull-headed monster that lurked inside a special maze on the island of Crete. The Athenians had to sacrifice seven boys and girls to the Minotaur every nine years, so the children of Athens were especially pleased to hear it had been killed.

PERSEUS AND MEDUSA

Perseus had to kill Medusa, a monstrous gorgon with snakes for hair. She was so ugly that anyone who looked at her instantly turned to stone. Perseus was helped by the gods Hermes and Athena. Perseus looked at Medusa's reflection in a magic shield when he cut off her head, so he wasn't turned to stone.

HELEN OF TROY

Paris, prince of Troy, had to judge which of three goddesses was the most beautiful. He chose Aphrodite, who promised him the world's most beautiful woman in return. Unfortunately, the world's most beautiful woman, Helen, was already married. When she ran off with Paris, it started the Trojan War between Greece and Troy, which lasted 10 years. It finally ended when the Greeks surprised the Trojans by leaping out of an enormous wooden horse that the Trojans thought was a gift.

DRACO

**HARD AS NAILS
RATING: 7.3**

Draco was an Athenian who laid down the law—and the criminals of Athens were in big trouble.

NOT A SOFTIE

Draco was born in the 600s BCE. We don't know very much about his life, but we can guess that his hobbies didn't include flower arranging, embroidery, and cuddling kittens. He is known for the laws that he wrote down for the constitution of Athens—and they are pretty fierce.

ROUGH JUSTICE

Before Draco, laws were in the hands of an elite group who passed judgment if a crime was committed. It was probably a very unfair system. The judges may have been making up things as they went along, or delivering harsh punishments to people just because they didn't like the look of them. Draco's laws, written around 621 BCE, made things clearer— but they were harsh. They gave death as the punishment for just about everything. If someone stole a cabbage, you might expect him to get a warning not to do it again or a minor punishment. But under Draco's laws, he'd be executed.

HARDOMETER

CUNNING: 6
COURAGE: 6
SURVIVAL SKILLS: 8
RUTHLESSNESS: 9

WORSE THAN DEATH

Apart from the moral question of whether it's right to kill people for minor offenses (or even major ones), if death is the punishment for both stealing and murder, a thief might be tempted to murder someone to avoid getting caught. However, these problems didn't seem to bother Draco. When he was questioned about the harshness of his punishments, he replied that he thought death was the correct punishment for the minor crimes, and he couldn't think of a more severe punishment for the serious ones. He did come up with another harsh punishment for people who owed money, however— as long as they belonged to a lower social class, they could be sold into slavery.

DRACONIAN RULES

It wasn't all bad. Well, it was mostly. But Draco did change things so that more people had a say in politics. Later, the politician Solon got rid of all Draco's laws, except the one for murder. Today, the word "draconian" describes rules that are unnecessarily harsh.

PERICLES

Pericles was a hard as nails general and politician who's remembered for making Athens the greatest city-state in Greece.

PERSIAN INVADERS

As a child, Pericles lived through troubled times: he was three when the Persians invaded Greece and were defeated at the Battle of Marathon (see page 46). Ten years later, Pericles might have been one of the children evacuated from Athens when it was pillaged by the Persians.

BUILDING UP ATHENS

The war with Persia was still going on when Pericles was first elected general of Athens in 458 BCE. When it finally ended in 449 BCE, Pericles decided to make Athens the most beautiful, and also the most powerful, of all the Greek city-states. In 447 BCE, work began on the Parthenon, the marble temple on top of the Acropolis that's still there today, along with many other impressive and expensive buildings. To pay for it, Pericles used the money given to Athens by its allies, the city-states in the Delian League.

HARDOMETER

CUNNING: 8
COURAGE: 7
SURVIVAL SKILLS: 6
RUTHLESSNESS: 8

SPARTA GETS ANGRY

Many people from the rest of the Delian League resented paying for all these buildings in Athens. Most resentful of all were the Spartans, and it was never a good idea to get on the wrong side of them. Pericles encouraged Athens to go to war with Sparta, and in 431 BCE they did.

SEA BATTLES

Pericles decided that the best way to win the war was to retreat inside the city walls and avoid land battles with Sparta. Instead, he would batter them at sea with the superior Athenian navy. At first, his plan seemed to be working. Pericles was especially good at giving speeches to make the Athenians confident about winning and proud of their polis. But then something happened that Pericles hadn't predicted . . .

PLAGUE AND PESTILENCE

Athens was struck by plague. The disease spread quickly, and dead bodies piled up in the streets as tens of thousands of people died. In 429 BCE, Pericles himself became one of the plague's victims. The war with Sparta continued for another 25 years, and in the end, Athens lost.

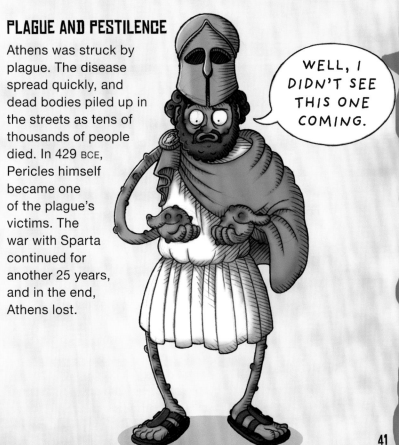

WELL, I DIDN'T SEE THIS ONE COMING.

PYRRHUS

Pyrrhus was a king who couldn't resist a fight, but he nearly lost everything when he tried to put a stop to the conquering Romans.

HARD AS NAILS RATING: 7.5

KING OF EPIRUS

Pyrrhus's father was the king of Epirus in northwestern Greece, but he was overthrown and killed when Pyrrhus was two. Luckily, Pyrrhus was whisked away to safety by a friendly relative. That same helpful relative invaded Epirus when Pyrrhus had grown up, and restored him to his throne.

HELP FROM PTOLEMY

You couldn't trust anyone in those days. While Pyrrhus was away at a wedding, someone stole his throne, so Pyrrhus went to stay with his sister and her husband, Demetrius (who happened to be the king of Asia). After a few battles and a marriage to the daughter of Ptolemy I, an Egyptian ruler, Pyrrhus sailed back to Epirus with a large army and navy supplied by Ptolemy. He quickly grabbed back his throne and, after killing his second cousin, became the sole king of Epirus once again.

MARAUDING ROMANS

By this time, the city of Rome had started to expand its territory by conquering the rest of Italy. A Greek city in southern Italy, Tarentum, called for Pyrrhus's help against the attacking Romans. Pyrrhus crossed the sea to Italy in 280 BCE with around 20,000 men—and a surprise.

HARDOMETER

CUNNING: 7
COURAGE: 8
SURVIVAL SKILLS: 7
RUTHLESSNESS: 8

PYRRHUS'S GIANT SURPRISE

Pyrrhus's surprise was war elephants. The Romans had never seen them before and were terrified. The giant animals helped Pyrrhus win. But the battle was a bloody one and Pyrrhus lost countless men. He's reported to have said that if he had another victory like that one it would be the end of him. Today, people still use the expression "Pyrrhic victory" to mean a victory won at a terrible cost.

MORE FIGHTING

Never one to say no to a fight, Pyrrhus also battled the Carthaginians, the Macedonians, and the Spartans. The Romans finally defeated Pyrrhus in 275 BCE. He was killed in a riot in Argos three years later.

CLEON

Cleon was a hard as nails
Athenian who absolutely hated
the Spartans, and led Athens into
bloody battles.

SPARTA AND PERICLES

The Peloponnesian War between Athens and Sparta was in
full swing by the time Cleon became an Athenian politician.
As well as hating the Spartans, Cleon really didn't like
Pericles (see page 40) either. It was Pericles's policy of
avoiding land battles with Sparta that annoyed him most.
Cleon accused Pericles of dishonest dealings with public
money and managed to get him removed from his position
of power, but only for a while. Finally, Pericles did Cleon a
favor by dying of the plague in 429 BCE.

MYTILENE

With Pericles out of the way, Cleon became the top
politician in Athens, but he soon had an uprising to deal
with. In 428 BCE the city-state of Mytilene on the island of
Lesbos rebelled. The Athenians quickly put a stop to it,
but Cleon wanted to teach them a lesson they wouldn't
forget. Proving his extreme ruthlessness,
he suggested that the entire male
population of Mytilene should
be executed. Luckily, other
Athenians had a say in what
happened. Cleon almost got his
way, but in the end, only about
a thousand Mytilene men
were killed.

HARDOMETER

CUNNING: 7
COURAGE: 9
SURVIVAL SKILLS: 6
RUTHLESSNESS: 10

CAPTURING SPARTANS

Cleon's finest hour came in 425 BCE, when he managed to capture Spartan troops who'd become stranded on the island of Sphacteria after the Battle of Pylos. He and the general Demosthenes brought the Spartans back to Athens. Cleon threatened to kill them all if Sparta invaded again—it had a nasty habit of invading every year and then going away to help with the harvest and deal with the slave population. His threat worked. The Athenians became much more confident about winning the war.

THE END OF THE WAR

But Cleon's triumph didn't last long. He was killed in 422 BCE, trying to recapture Amphipolis, a city once controlled by Athens that the Spartans had captured. The Spartans got him in the end. After he died, the Athenian general Nicias negotiated a peace deal with the Spartans, which would have really annoyed Cleon. The fighting stopped—but only for seven years.

WANTED

PHEIDIPPIDES

One of the toughest ancient Greeks of them all isn't famous for conquering or fighting, but for running.

SPARTAN HELP

The Persians arrived in Greece in 490 BCE, intent on making as much of it as possible a part of the Persian Empire. Their army assembled on the plains near the city of Marathon, about 25 miles (40 km) from Athens. When the Athenian army arrived to meet them, they could see they were outnumbered. So they sent a messenger, Pheidippides, to Sparta to ask for help. After he'd run all the way there, the Spartans said they'd help, but not right away. Heaving a big sigh, Pheidippides turned around and headed back with the news, a round trip of about 155 miles (250 km) in two days.

THE BATTLE OF MARATHON

The Athenians decided to attack the Persians without Spartan help. The Athenian general Miltiades probably came up with the clever tactics that encircled the Persians, defeated them, and forced them to run back to their ships on the coast. Many of them drowned in the swamps on the way, but plenty of them succeeded in making it to the ships and, despite the Athenians' best efforts, most of the ships headed out to sea.

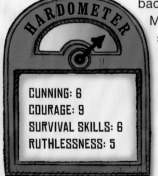

HARDOMETER

CUNNING: 6
COURAGE: 9
SURVIVAL SKILLS: 6
RUTHLESSNESS: 5

MARATHON TO ATHENS

The victorious Athenians knew that if the Persian ships reached Athens before they did, the Athenians might hand over the city to the marauding invaders, assuming that the Persians had won. The story goes that Pheidippides ran the 25 miles (40 km) to Athens with the news of the Athenian victory as fast as he could—despite the fact he'd just run 153 miles (245 km), and fought in a major battle. But Pheidippides was hard as nails. He made it in record time, gave the Athenians the good news, then dropped dead of exhaustion. The Athenian army arrived later, and the thwarted Persians headed for home.

MODERN MARATHONS

Pheidippides's run from Marathon to Athens might not be true, but marathon races today are based on the distance between the two cities. Every year, a 153-mile (245 km) race called the Spartathlon recreates Pheidippides's longer run to ask for Spartan help.

TO ATHENS

XERXES THE GREAT

King Xerxes I was a Persian emperor intent on grabbing Greece. Although he won battles and pillaged Athens, he never succeeded in making Greece part of his empire.

INHERITING AN EMPIRE

Xerxes was the son of Darius the Great (see page 34), and he came to the throne when his father died in 486 BCE. From the very start, he made sure everyone knew he was ruthless, fierce, and, most importantly, in charge. He began by battering Egypt and Babylon, which were both under Persian control.

WHIPPING UP A STORM

Next, Xerxes turned his attention to one of his father's favorite activities: invading Greece. He amassed an army and navy and made boat bridges across the Hellespont, the narrow stretch of sea that links the Mediterranean Sea with the sea of Marmaris. A storm destroyed the bridges, and the story goes that Xerxes was so furious, he looked for someone to blame. He decided the sea was responsible, so he had it whipped with chains to teach it a lesson. It must have worked, because Xerxes's men remade the bridges and the Persian army crossed over into Greece.

PILLAGING PERSIANS

The first major battle with the allied Greeks was at the narrow mountain pass of Thermopylae. The Persians won after a long and bloody battle, but they suffered heavy losses at the hands of Spartan leader and self-sacrificing toughie, Leonidas (see page 16). Xerxes managed to invade and occupy Attica—the area surrounding Athens—and pillaged Athens itself in 480 BCE, wrecking the Acropolis and setting fire to Athenian monuments.

PERSIANS GO HOME

Despite making himself extremely unpopular throughout Greece, Xerxes the Great never became its emperor. The Persian fleet was defeated at the Battle of Salamis, which was the beginning of the end for Persian invasion plans. Xerxes lost interest in grabbing Greece after that, and eventually the Persians left it completely.

MURDER

Xerxes spent the rest of his life in the Persian cities of Susa and Persepolis. But rampaging conquerors rarely get to live out their days in peace, and in 465 BCE Xerxes was murdered by treacherous members of his royal court.

PELOPIDAS

Pelopidas was a Theban warrior who created one of the fiercest fighting units in history, the Sacred Band of Thebes. They beat the toughest Greek warriors of all, the Spartans.

THEBES AND SPARTA

Around 20 years after the end of the Peloponnesian War, Thebes was a wealthy city-state and an ally of Sparta. Pelopidas fought alongside the Spartans as a young man in 385 BCE, against the Arcadians at the Battle of Mantinea. He was badly wounded but saved by his pal Epaminondas.

SPARTA TAKES OVER

Thebes and Sparta didn't stay friends for long. With the help of a group of traitorous Thebans, Spartans captured the fortress of Thebes, the Cadmea, and took over the city-state. Pelopidas went into exile in Athens, where he spent his time persuading other Theban exiles to drive the Spartans out of Thebes. In 379 BCE he led a brave band of rebels against the new Theban rulers, killed them all, and kicked out the Spartans.

HARDOMETER

CUNNING: 9
COURAGE: 10
SURVIVAL SKILLS: 8
RUTHLESSNESS: 9

THE SACRED BAND OF THEBES

Sparta planned its revenge, but Pelopidas was ready for it. He formed an elite fighting force of 300 young men, known as the Sacred Band of Thebes. They were highly trained warriors, tough as old boots, and united in their aim to defend Thebes or die trying. Pelopidas and his men defeated Spartan troops when they met at the Battle of Tegyra, which only made the Spartans more determined. A 10,000-strong Spartan army marched on Thebes in 371 BCE. The Theban army was commanded by Pelopidas's old friend Epaminondas. Pelopidas led the Sacred Band, and despite being outnumbered by the Spartans, the Thebans won.

TYRANT TROUBLE

Pelopidas's reputation for being hard as nails meant that Thessaly asked for his help against the tyrant Alexander of Pherae, who was to become very troublesome for Pelopidas. His army defeated Alexander, and drove the Macedonians out of Thessaly.

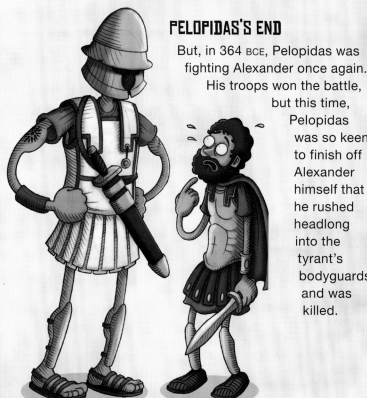

PELOPIDAS'S END

But, in 364 BCE, Pelopidas was fighting Alexander once again. His troops won the battle, but this time, Pelopidas was so keen to finish off Alexander himself that he rushed headlong into the tyrant's bodyguards and was killed.

HIPPOCRATES

Hippocrates was a doctor who made such an impact that, 2,500 years later, new doctors still swear an oath named after him.

TRAVELING DOCTOR

Hippocrates was born around 460 BCE on the island of Kos. He traveled around Greece tending to sick people and training new doctors. His methods made him famous, and doctors who came after him continued to use his ideas for treating patients. He was one of the first doctors to realize that diseases had natural causes. Most people believed that they were caused by the gods or evil spirits. Before Hippocrates, sick people would probably be taken to a temple or given some lucky charms, neither of which was likely to make them any better.

GETTING IT WRONG

Hippocrates did get one or two things wrong. He thought that diseases were caused by a bad diet, so he prescribed medicine to make patients sick and get rid of the disease-causing food. He also believed there were four "humors" in the human body that had to be kept in balance. Treatment might mean draining a patient's blood to keep the humors balanced. Doctors were still doing that up until about 200 years ago!

HARDOMETER

CUNNING: 4
COURAGE: 9
SURVIVAL SKILLS: 8
RUTHLESSNESS: 4

GETTING IT RIGHT

Hippocrates did get a lot of things right, though. He was the first person to make systematic

observations of diseases and keep careful records—
methods that sound obvious and are used today, but
weren't at that time. He was the first to describe diseases
including pneumonia, malaria, tetanus, and tuberculosis.
He also made a point of getting to know his patients and
treating them sympathetically, which helped some people
get better.

THE DOCTOR WILL SNIFF YOU NOW

Hippocrates must have been made of strong stuff,
because some of his methods
were not for the faint-
hearted: he tasted
patients' urine and
earwax, examined
their sweat to see
if it was sticky,
and studied and
smelled poo,
snot, and vomit.
Despite that, he
lived until he was
85, and became
the most famous
(and brave)
doctor ever.

I SUSPECT
THE COMMON
COLD!

PISISTRATUS

Pisistratus slashed, bludgeoned, plotted, and ambushed his way into becoming the tyrant of Athens.

HARD AS NAILS
RATING: 8.5

POLITICS

In the 500s BCE there were bitter arguments about how Athens should be run. Two powerful rivals, Lycurgus and Megacles, opposed one another. Around 565 BCE, when Athens was at war with Megara, Pisistratus became famous for capturing the enemy's harbor. He made the most of his popularity by setting up his own rival group.

TYRANT OF ATHENS

As a dramatic and bloody publicity stunt, Pisistratus slashed his own body and drove into Athens's marketplace to show everyone how his enemies had wounded him. The trick worked: the people of Athens voted in favor of Pisistratus having bodyguards armed with clubs. Cunning Pisistratus lost no time in using the club-wielding men to help him take over the Acropolis by force. He was now the first tyrant of Athens—a leader who was in charge because he'd fought his way to the top.

HARDOMETER

CUNNING: 9
COURAGE: 8
SURVIVAL SKILLS: 9
RUTHLESSNESS: 8

EXILED AND ANGRY

But it didn't last long. Pisistratus's two main rivals, Lycurgus and Megacles, managed to overthrow him after about a year. Pisistratus went to live in exile in northern Greece, where he spent his time growing rich from silver and gold mines.

He gained support from like-minded rich people, and began plotting and putting his own personal army together.

SURPRISE ATTACK

In 546 BCE Pisistratus marched toward Athens with his army and launched an attack on the Athenian army just when they were least expecting it—in the heat of midday, when half of them were asleep. He quickly defeated the Athenian army and marched into Athens, becoming its tyrant once again.

POPULAR PISISTRATUS

Once in charge, Pisistratus began many impressive and useful building projects, encouraged poetry and music, and—unusual for a tyrant—didn't wage any wars. True, he did take hostages from powerful families and keep them on the island of Naxos, and he kept a very scary bodyguard. But generally Pisistratus was popular, and he remained Athens's tyrant until he died in 527 BCE.

PERDICCAS

HARD AS NAILS RATING: 7.3

Perdiccas was a Macedonian general who ruled the huge empire created by Alexander the Great. Perdiccas was ruthless and tough, but became too big-headed for his own good.

GENERAL PERDICCAS

Perdiccas was one of Alexander the Great's (see page 12) most trusted generals. He earned a reputation as a brilliant warrior while Alexander's army was battering Thebes into submission in 335 BCE, but he was badly wounded there. He went on to command Alexander's cavalry campaigns in India.

ENORMOUS EMPIRE

Alexander died in 323 BCE when he was only 32, leaving an empire that stretched from Egypt to India. Perdiccas thought he should be the man to rule it. Alexander's brother was made king alongside Alexander's unborn baby, but because he wasn't healthy enough to rule and Alexander's baby was clearly too young, Perdiccas got his way and became regent, ruling in their place.

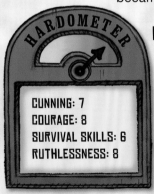

HARDOMETER

CUNNING: 7
COURAGE: 8
SURVIVAL SKILLS: 6
RUTHLESSNESS: 8

REVOLTING GENERALS

Many people didn't like the idea of Perdiccas running things, especially since he planned to marry Alexander's sister, which meant he would have more claim to rule the empire than anyone else. But first, there was conquering to do.

Cappadocia (in modern-day Turkey) was one of the few places Alexander hadn't conquered, so Perdiccas invaded it right away. He was expecting help from Antigonus, the governor of Phrygia, but it never came. Perdiccas summoned Antigonus to stand trial for disobedience but, sensibly, Antigonus ran away to Perdiccas's rivals, three men called Antipater, Craterus, and Ptolemy. They had all been Alexander's generals as well. They agreed to revolt against Perdiccas.

MUTINY

Perdiccas left a friend to defend Asia against Antipater and Craterus while he marched on Ptolemy in Egypt. Ptolemy's army stopped him from crossing the Nile, and some of Perdiccas's men were swept away in the river. Perdiccas's troops had had enough: he was a harsh leader, and now they were stuck on the banks of the Nile because of him. Finally, three of Perdiccas's officers assassinated him.

HARD AS NAILS IN ANCIENT GREECE TIMELINE

AROUND 800–500 BCE

People had been living in Greece for thousands of years, and different civilizations came and went. In this period, Greece expanded into colonies around the Mediterranean, the first Olympic Games were held, and Athens became the biggest and richest city-state.

600s BCE

Draco, who made some very harsh laws in Athens, was born some time in this century

570 BCE

Cleisthenes, the leader who introduced democracy to Athens, was born around this date.

550 BCE

Persian ruler Darius the Great was born. He would later invade Greece.

527 BCE

Pisistratus, the tyrant of Athens, died.

524 BCE

Themistocles was born around this date. He created a powerful Athenian navy.

519 BCE

Xerxes the Great, the Persian emperor, was born around this date.

AROUND 500–336 BCE

This period is known as the Classical Age, when Greek culture flourished.

499–449 BCE

The Persian Wars between Persia and Greece lasted 50 years. The allied Greek city-states eventually drove out the Persians.

495 BCE

Athenian general Pericles was born around this date.
He led Athens in the war with Sparta, and is remembered
for making Athens great.

490 BCE

Pheidippides died after running the first-ever marathon.

480 BCE

Leonidas, the self-sacrificing Spartan warrior, died fighting
the Persians.

470 BCE

The philosopher Socrates was born around this date.
Agreed to poison himself as punishment by the court for
disrespecting the gods.

460 BCE

Famous doctor Hippocrates was born around this date.

450 BCE

Alcibiades, the general who fought for both Athens and Sparta,
was born around this date.

431–404 BCE

The Peloponnesian Wars were fought between Athens and the Peloponnesian League. In the end, Sparta and its allies in the league won.

422 BCE

Athenian general Cleon died in battle against the Spartans.

395 BCE

Spartan leader Lysander died. He commanded the fleet that finally ended the Peloponnesian War.

371 BCE

Thebes defeated Sparta to become the leading Greek city-state.

365 BCE

Perdiccas was born around this date. He was one of Alexander the Great's generals. Perdiccas went on to command huge parts of the empire.

364 BCE

Theban warrior Pelopidas died fighting the tyrant Alexander of Pherae.

356 BCE

Unstoppable conqueror Alexander the Great was born.

338 BCE

Philip II of Macedonia became ruler of Greece.

319 BCE

Pyrrhus, king of Epirus, was born. He defeated the conquering Romans, but at a huge cost.

290 BCE

Archimedes, the inventor and mathematician, was born around this date.

146 BCE

Greece became part of the Roman Empire.

415 CE

Brilliant mathematician and astronomer Hypatia was killed.

LEARNING MORE

BOOKS

Benoit, Peter. *The Ancient World: Ancient Greece*. New York: Scholastic, 2013.

Pearson, Anne. *Ancient Greece*. London: Dorling Kindersley, 2014.

Peppas, Lynn. *Life in Ancient Greece*. Crabtree Publishing, 2005.

EDUCATIONAL WEBSITES

Ancient Greece, The British Museum: **www.ancientgreece.co.uk**

Ancient Greeks, BBC History: **www.bbc.co.uk/schools/primaryhistory/ancient_greeks**

Greece History Timeline, Time for Kids: **www.timeforkids.com/destination/greece/history-timeline**

GLOSSARY

ACROPOLIS The city center of ancient Athens

AGOGE A military boarding school where Spartan men trained to be warriors

ALLIANCE An agreement between different countries or groups to work together in order to achieve something

ARCHON The top political job in ancient Athens

ASSASSINATED Murdered in a surprise attack (usually for political reasons)

BESIEGED Surrounded by enemy forces

BLOCKADED Closed off by enemy forces so that people cannot enter or leave

CLASSICAL AGE About 500-336 BCE, when Greek culture fourished

COLONIES Territories that are under the control of another state or country

CONSTITUTION A set of national laws according to which a country is governed

CORRUPTING Ruining someone's good character by encouraging them to do something wrong

DELIAN LEAGUE An association of Greek city-states

DEMOCRACY A form of government where leaders are chosen by the people of the state or country

EXILE Being banned from your home country

FLEET A group of warships

HEMLOCK A highly poisonous plant

HUMORS The four fluids of the human body (black bile, yellow bile, phlegm, and blood). An imbalance of the humors was thought to cause ill health

IMPOSTER A person who pretends to be someone else

MASSACRED Brutally killed

MEGALOMANIAC A person who believes they have great power and importance

PENINSULA A piece of land sticking out from the mainland that is surrounded by water on three sides

PERSECUTED Ill-treated due to political or religious beliefs

PLAGUE A deadly infectious disease

POLIS An ancient Greek city-state

REGENT Someone temporarily acting as a head of state

THWARTED Stopped from doing something

TYRANT An absolute ruler in Greece; also, a harsh and cruel leader

INDEX